STAR WARS

THE FORCE AWAKENS

WRITTEN BY ADAM BRAY, DAVID FENTIMAN, AND COLE HORTON

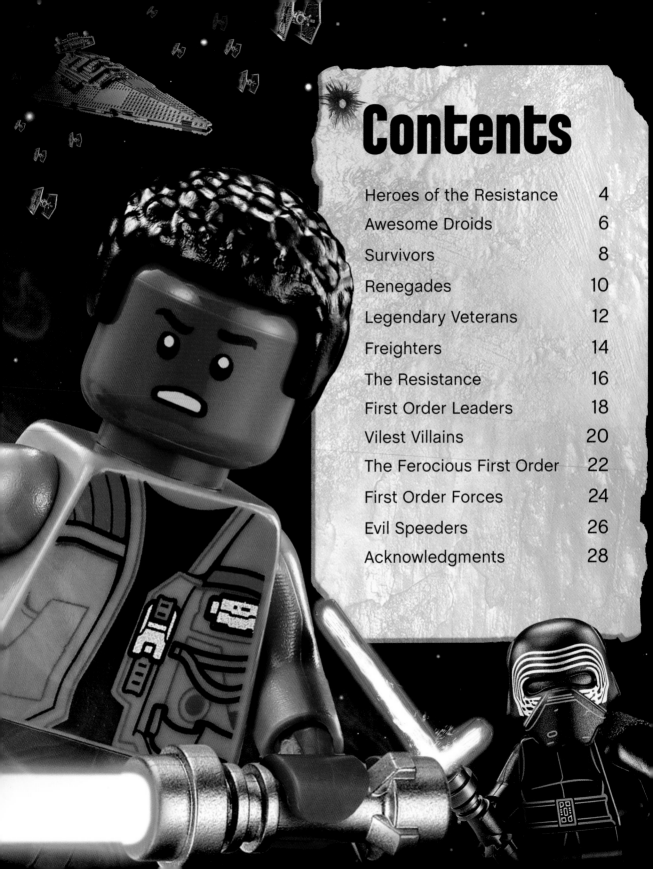

Contents

INTRODUCTION

A galaxy in turmoil. Again.

The First Order is terrifying the people of the galaxy. Stormtrooper armies are massing for battle. Their mysterious leaders lurk in the shadows.

Many heroes of old have been called back into action. What secrets from the past can they teach us? What lost wisdom is there to discover? Which events have shaped the galaxy over the course of history? Will the light side triumph once more?

It is time to find out.

These brave minifigures are the latest heroes of the LEGO *Star Wars* universe. Rey, Finn, Poe, and BB-8 are all part of the Resistance. They will have to work together to defeat the terrifying First Order.

Heroes of the Resistance
ENEMIES OF THE FIRST ORDER

DATA FILE

NAME: Rey
YEAR: 2015
FIRST SET: 75099
Rey's Speeder
NO. OF SETS: 2
PIECES: 5
ACCESSORIES: Quarterstaff

Great Goggles
Rey's headscarf is unique to this minifigure. Her goggles are scavenged lenses from an Imperial stormtrooper's helmet.

LEGO Quarterstaff weapon built from two lightsaber hilt pieces connected by a bar

Unique printing on legs and hips

Satchel for tools

DATA FILE

NAME: Finn
YEAR: 2015
FIRST SET: 75105
Millennium Falcon
NO. OF SETS: 2
PIECES: 4
ACCESSORIES: Blaster

Resistance jacket "borrowed" from Poe Dameron

Double-printed head piece has two expressions: determined focus and anxious concern

Short blaster

Stormtrooper temperature-control body glove

Brown belt detail continues around the back of the torso

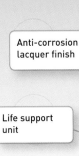

Anti-corrosion lacquer finish

Resistance symbol on Poe's helmet

Life support unit

Expert Pilot
Poe used to be part of the New Republic's starfighter forces, but he left to join the Resistance. His code name is Black Leader, and he heroically leads the Resistance pilots into battle.

DATA FILE

NAME: Poe Dameron
YEAR: 2015
FIRST SET: 75102
Poe's X-wing Fighter
NO. OF SETS: 2
PIECES: 4
ACCESSORIES: Blaster

Ejection harness

Main photoreceptor

Stainless inoxium

Holoprojector array

DATA FILE

NAME: BB-8
YEAR: 2015
FIRST SET: 75102
Poe's X-wing Fighter
NO. OF SETS: 2
PIECES: 2
ACCESSORIES: None

Silver and orange printing shows circular tool-bay disks

Loyal droid
BB-8 is Poe's astromech droid. Onboard Poe's X-wing, BB-8 helps Poe by repairing damage, plotting routes through space, and managing the ship's systems.

Poe's X-wing Fighter (set 75102)
Poe leads the attack on Starkiller Base in his customized T-70 X-wing fighter. It is called *Black One* and is BB-8's favorite ship.

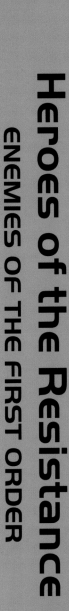

AWESOME DROIDS

THEY ARE PILOTS, portable power chargers, mechanics, medics, and more. There is a robotic droid for nearly every job you can imagine!

TOP 3
Reasons why droids are the best workers

1 THEY NEVER STOP FOR LUNCH

2 THEY NEVER ASK FOR A RAISE

3 THEY CAN LEARN NEW SKILLS BY DOWNLOADING NEW PROGRAMMING

REALLY?!

Some people don't treat droids kindly. The Mos Eisley Cantina bartender doesn't allow droids to come inside because they don't buy drinks!

BRICK-SIZED FACT

The GNK droid's body is used in other LEGO sets as a mailbox!

Q & A
Which droids are good in an emergency?

2-1B is a skilled medical droid. He is programmed to perform all kinds of medical tasks, like bandaging wounds and replacing lost hands.

Surgical assistant droids help doctors to do their work, and monitor the bacta tanks in which heroes quickly hea[l]

HELPFUL DROIDS

GNK DROID

GNK (pronounced "gonk") droids supply power to just about anything, including other droids.

MOUSE DROID

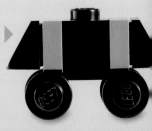

Mouse droids zoom around the halls of the Death Star and Star Destroyers, cleaning the floors as they go.

THE UNIVERSE IN UNITS

4

The number of manipulator arms on a treadwell repair droid

WOW!

A BB-8 droid's rolling, circular body allows it to travel at much faster speeds than most other droid models.

FORCE FACTS

Name: BB-8

Affiliation: Resistance

Owner: Poe Dameron

Droid type: Astromech

Skills: Navigation, ship maintenance, piloting, data storage

DROID KIDNAPPERS

Pesky Jawas kidnap droids and sell them to the highest bidder! The Jawa transfer crane lifts droids by their heads into their hulking sandcrawler.

SURVIVORS

THE PLANETS JAKKU AND TATOOINE are difficult places to live! They're dangerously hot, and there's little water. Strange creatures and humans survive in these desert environments by adapting in unique ways.

FORCE NUMBERS ● ● ● ●

3,296 pieces
Included in Sandcrawler (set 75059)

30kph (18.6mph)
Maximum speed of a Jawa sandcrawler

6 minifigures
Featured in Jabba's Sail Barge (set 7962), including R2-D2 with a drinks tray

3 sets
Include Jawa minifigures

FORCE KNOWLEDGE

DESERT THIEVES
Fearsome Sand People survive in the desert by raiding settlements and stealing supplies from farmers, traders, and unlucky travelers!

NO WAY!
Jawas have a reputation for being dirty and smelly. Some people believe that, underneath their hoods, Jawas look like rats.

"DISGUSTING CREATURES!"
C-3PO ABOUT JAWAS

Q&A
How do you travel in the desert?

AT TOP SPEED
Luke learned to fly by piloting a T-16 skyhopper through the canyons of Tatooine.

ON THE BACK OF A DEWBACK
Dewbacks carry people and cargo on their backs. When the sun goes down, these lizards slow to a standstill.

IN STYLE
Jabba the Hutt carries guards, slaves, and prisoners across the sand dunes aboard his personal barge.

JAKKU SCAVENGER

Rey works as a scavenger, going into spooky old starship wrecks looking for anything valuable. She works for a cruel junk dealer named Unkar Plutt, who uses his thugs to boss Rey and the other scavengers around.

STRANGE

Tatooine is so dry, citizens have to draw water from the air. Luke's Aunt Beru and Uncle Owen own a moisture farm that uses vaporators to collect water.

AWESOME!

Unkar Plutt's henchmen wear scary masks to hide their identities. They aren't very smart, and Unkar mainly uses them to threaten people.

FORCE FACTS

Name: Rey

Occupation: Scavenger

Affiliation: Resistance

Species: Human

Homeworld: Jakku

Abilities: Fighting, scavenging, mechanics, the Force

ICK-SIZED FACT

6 Skyhopper et 75081) is e first set to re a Tatooine omp rat.

THE UNIVERSE IN UNITS
846MPH
Maximum speed of a T-16 skyhopper

"FOLLOW ME!"
REY TO FINN

RENEGADES

A RENEGADE is a person who changes their path in life, deserting one organization to join another. There are some people in the galaxy, like Finn, whose conscience leads them to abandon evil paths for more honorable ones. Others, like Count Dooku, Pong Krell, or Anakin Skywalker, turn to the dark side.

FORCE KNOWLEDGE

JEDI PATHS

Count Dooku begins a line of Jedi with remarkable career paths. Dooku leaves the Jedi and becomes a Sith. His Padawan, Qui-Gon Jinn, is very independent. Less so is Qui-Gon's student, Obi-Wan Kenobi. Obi-Wan's Padawan, Anakin Skywalker, becomes the evil Darth Vader.

FORCE FACTS

Name: Finn

Occupation: Former stormtroope Resistance fighter

Affiliation: Resistance

Species: Human

Abilities: Blaster combat, lightsaber fighting

FORCE NUMBERS ● ● ● ●

3 versions
Of the Count Dooku minifigure

2 minifigures
Wear stolen stormtrooper armor—Han Solo and Luke Skywalker

1 set
Features Pong Krell (set 75004)

NO WAY!

Jedi General Pong Krell sends clones to their deaths without any reason—except perhaps, to please evil Darth Sidious, whom he wishes to join!

TOP 3
Daring disguises

1

LEIA ORGANA

As Boushh the bounty hunter, Leia deceives Jabba to enter his palace and rescue Han Solo.

2

LANDO CALRISSIAN

Lando secretly works as one of Jabba's skiff guards to help Leia, and then Luke, escape the gangster.

3

LUKE SKYWALKER

Luke wears stolen stormtrooper armor to get past the Death Star security forces and rescue Leia.

FORCE KNOWLEDGE

KANAN JARRUS

When his Jedi Master, Depa Billaba, is defeated by clone troopers, Padawan Caleb Dume abandons his Jedi education. He changes his name to Kanan Jarrus and goes into hiding before eventually joining the fight against the Empire.

> **" I'VE GOT**
> # NOTHING
> **TO FIGHT FOR."**
> FINN

REALLY?!

Finn borrowed Poe's Resistance fighter jacket after the pair of them crash-landed on the planet Jakku.

Legendary Veterans
NOBLE HEROES

It seems that a hero's job is never finished. Luckily, Han, Ackbar, Leia, and Maz have over 1,000 years of experience between them. They are ready to defend the galaxy against the evil First Order in any way they can.

Gray hair piece is the same as General Airen Cracken's

Nerf-leather jacket

Han still uses his favorite DL-44 blaster even though better weapons are available

DATA FILE

NAME: Han Solo
YEAR: 2015
FIRST SET: 75105
Millennium Falcon
NO. OF SETS: 1
PIECES: 4
ACCESSORIES: Blaster

Still smiling
The expression on the reverse of Han's double-sid head piece reveals that his confident grin has not left h

DATA FILE

NAME: Admiral Ackbar
YEAR: 2016
FIRST SET: 75140
Resistance Troop Transporter
NO. OF SETS: 1
PIECES: 3
ACCESSORIES: Blaster, mug

Ackbar's unique head piece is made from hard ABS plastic

Ackbar's skin is more mottled than his previous minifigure version

Admiral's rank badge

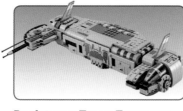

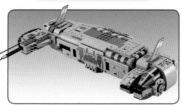

Resistance Troop Transporter (set 75140)
It is only in a LEGO *Star Wars* set that Admiral Ackbar would join the troops on Takodana. Normally, this Admiral would focus on directing the troops from the Resistance's command center.

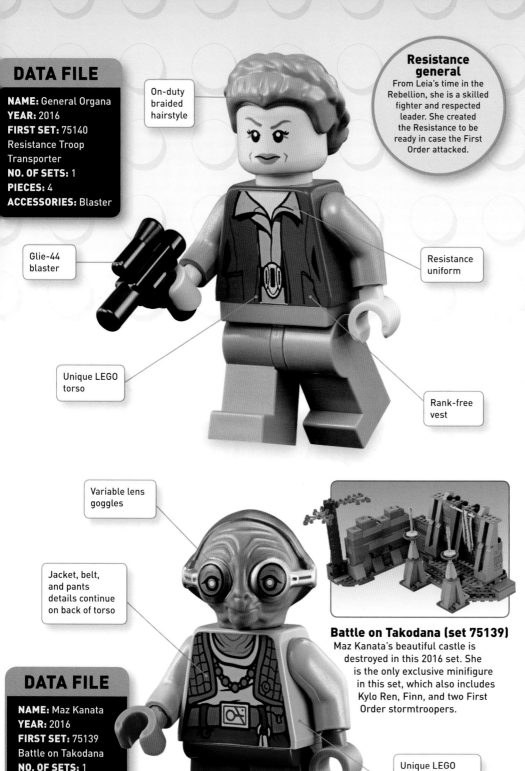

DATA FILE

NAME: General Organa
YEAR: 2016
FIRST SET: 75140
Resistance Troop
Transporter
NO. OF SETS: 1
PIECES: 4
ACCESSORIES: Blaster

On-duty braided hairstyle

Resistance general
From Leia's time in the Rebellion, she is a skilled fighter and respected leader. She created the Resistance to be ready in case the First Order attacked.

Glie-44 blaster

Resistance uniform

Unique LEGO torso

Rank-free vest

Variable lens goggles

Jacket, belt, and pants details continue on back of torso

Battle on Takodana (set 75139)
Maz Kanata's beautiful castle is destroyed in this 2016 set. She is the only exclusive minifigure in this set, which also includes Kylo Ren, Finn, and two First Order stormtroopers.

DATA FILE

NAME: Maz Kanata
YEAR: 2016
FIRST SET: 75139
Battle on Takodana
NO. OF SETS: 1
PIECES: 3
ACCESSORIES: None

Unique LEGO torso shows Maz's clothes that she has knitted herself

13

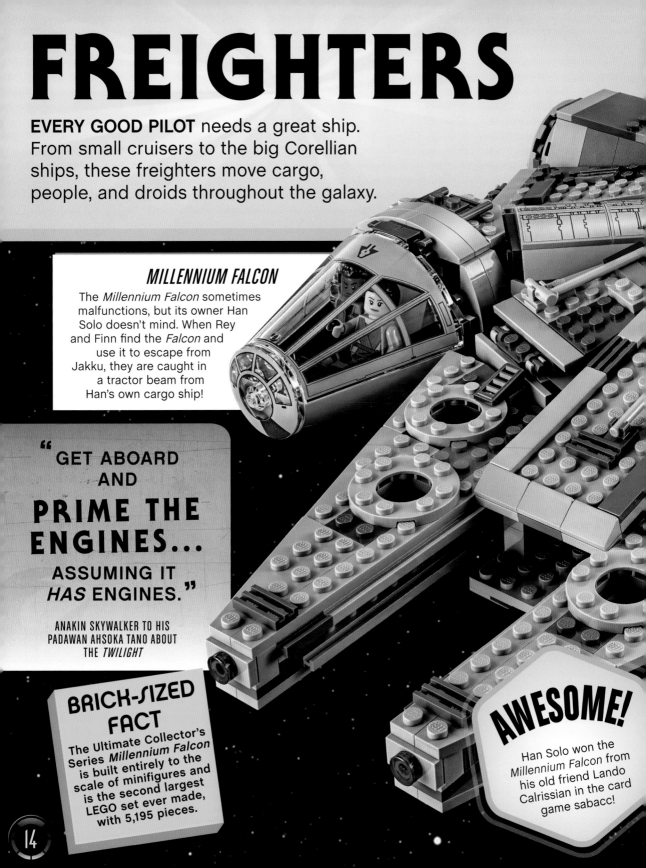

FREIGHTERS

EVERY GOOD PILOT needs a great ship. From small cruisers to the big Corellian ships, these freighters move cargo, people, and droids throughout the galaxy.

MILLENNIUM FALCON

The *Millennium Falcon* sometimes malfunctions, but its owner Han Solo doesn't mind. When Rey and Finn find the *Falcon* and use it to escape from Jakku, they are caught in a tractor beam from Han's own cargo ship!

" **GET ABOARD AND**

PRIME THE ENGINES...

ASSUMING IT *HAS* ENGINES. "

ANAKIN SKYWALKER TO HIS PADAWAN AHSOKA TANO ABOUT THE *TWILIGHT*

BRICK-SIZED FACT

The Ultimate Collector's Series *Millennium Falcon* is built entirely to the scale of minifigures and is the second largest LEGO set ever made, with 5,195 pieces.

AWESOME!

Han Solo won the *Millennium Falcon* from his old friend Lando Calrissian in the card game sabacc!

311

Pages of instructions for building the Ultimate Collector's Series *Millennium Falcon* set

REALLY?!

Freighter pilots pass the time by playing games like holochess. But it's no fun playing against a Wookiee—they have been known to become extremely angry when they lose!

NEW OWNERS

Han Solo lost the *Millennium Falcon* after the Rebellion was over. It ended up in the hands of the vicious Jakku junk dealer Unkar Plutt.

FAMOUS REBEL CORELLIAN FREIGHTERS

TANTIVE IV ▼

Senator Bail Organa is the proud owner of this ship, with Captain Antilles as pilot. Unfortunately for the rebels, it is later captured by Darth Vader!

THE *GHOST* ▲

Owned by the rebel Hera Syndulla and home base to her loyal crew, the *Ghost* has two huge rocket boosters and an escape pod in case of emergencies.

THE *TWILIGHT* ▲

Anakin Skywalker found the *Twilight* on a landing platform on the planet Teth. He gave it much needed upgrades, including three blaster cannons and a tow hook for hauling large cargo.

THE RESISTANCE

THE RESISTANCE WAS formed by General Leia Organa to keep watch on the activities of the mysterious First Order. She leads this group of freedom fighters in protecting the galaxy from the powers of the dark side.

BRICK-SIZED FACT

Poe's minifigure flies two different X-wing LEGO sets: a blue Resistance X-wing and his unique black and orange X-wing.

REALLY?!

Poe flies a standard blue Resistance X-wing before it is destroyed on Jakku. He later flies a customized X-wing.

STRANGE

Poe first flew a starship when he was just six years old!

RESISTANCE TROOPS

◄ SOLDIERS
The Resistance's soldiers do not have fancy armor, but they are braver than any stormtrooper.

GROUND CREW ►
The pilots may win the glory, but they'd be stuck on the ground without the handy ship mechanics.

PILOTS
The Resistance's X-wing pilots are elite fliers, who take the battle to the First Order.

DROIDS ►
Many astromech droids serve bravely in the Resistance, helping pilots fly their ships.

TOP 3
Resistance leaders

1 **GENERAL LEIA ORGANA**
Leia puts her royal title behind her, and leaves the New Republic Senate to lead the Resistance as its general.

2 **ADMIRAL STATURA**
Admiral Statura serves as Leia's second-in-command. He fought in the Rebellion when he was still a teenager, and is an old friend of Leia.

3 **ADMIRAL ACKBAR**
Admiral Ackbar served with Leia during the Rebellion. He came out of retirement to battle the First Order.

NO WAY!
Pilot Poe Dameron's parents fought in the Rebel Alliance, so he followed in their footsteps.

FORCE FACTS
Name: Poe Dameron

Occupation: Starfighter pilot

Affiliation: Resistance

Species: Human

Homeworld: Yavin 4

Personal idol: General Leia Organa

These monstrous minifigures lead the First Order's forces. The First Order is an evil group that wants to take over the LEGO *Star Wars* galaxy. While Hux and other officers may command from afar, Kylo Ren and Captain Phasma join their troops in action. The Resistance had best watch out!

First Order Leaders
VILE VILLAINS

DATA FILE

NAME: Kylo Ren
YEAR: 2015
FIRST SET: 75104
Kylo Ren's Shuttle
NO. OF SETS: 2
PIECES: 6
ACCESSORIES:
Lightsaber

Torn cape singed from many battles

Combat helmet based on the equipment of the Knights of Ren

Kylo's unique lightsaber, with two crossguard blades, is similar to ancient lightsabers

Under the hood
In the 2015 Kylo Ren's Shuttle set (75104), Kylo's head piece is not printed with his face, but is printed with his helmet instead. Kylo can either wear a hood over this head piece or wear his more detailed helmet accessory.

DATA FILE

NAME: Captain Phasma
YEAR: 2015
FIRST SET: 75103
First Order Transporter
NO. OF SETS: 1
PIECES: 5
ACCESSORIES: Blaster

Unique silver metallic blaster

Helmet conceals a plain LEGO head that does not have any face printing

First Order command cape

Ammunition holders

Chrome commander
Captain Phasma leads the First Order stormtroopers. Her armor is coated in salvaged chronium from a Naboo ship that once belonged to Emperor Palpatine.

General's command cap with First Order insignia

Great general
Son of a high-ranking officer in the Galactic Empire, the ambitious and ruthless General Hux is a busy man. He is the commander of Starkiller Base and in charge of the First Order's armies.

Unique head piece has a stern expression

Gaberwool greatcoat detailing continues on the back of Hux's torso

DATA FILE

NAME: General Hux
YEAR: 2015
FIRST SET: 75104
Kylo Ren's Shuttle
NO. OF SETS: 1
PIECES: 4
ACCESSORIES:
Blaster pistol

Officer's buckle

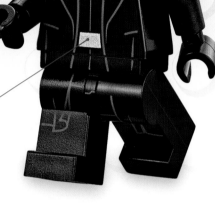

Humorless face is exclusive to this minifigure

Kylo Ren's Shuttle (set 75104)
This First Order officer is one of six minifigures to come with this set. She helps to operate Kylo's shuttle which carries Kylo to his latest mission.

Rank Cylinders

Quadnoculars used to spot enemy fighters

Belt printing continues on back of torso

DATA FILE

NAME: First Order Officer
YEAR: 2014
FIRST SET: 75104
Kylo Ren's Shuttle
NO. OF SETS: 1
PIECES: 4
ACCESSORIES:
Binoculars

VILEST VILLAINS

FORCE NUMBERS ●●●

3,152 bricks
In Super Star Destroyer (set 10221)

83 years old
Dooku's age when he is defeated by Anakin Skywalker

9 horns
Crown Darth Maul's head

6 sets
Include General Grievous minifigures

THE SITH ARE among the most powerful foes in the galaxy. Sith supporters can be found throughout the Empire, even in its highest ranks.

> " LET THE **HATE** FLOW THROUGH YOU. "
>
> DARTH SIDIOUS TO LUKE SKYWALKER

STRANGE

After Darth Maul is cut in two with a lightsaber, he survives as a cyborg-like spider for a while, later receiving two new mechanical legs.

THE EVOLUTION OF ... DARTH VADER

PODRACER PILOT
Young Anakin Skywalker grows up on Tatooine. He meets Jedi Master Qui-Gon Jinn, who sees great potential in him.

JEDI PADAWAN
Qui-Gon's Padawan, Obi-Wan Kenobi, trains Anakin in the ways of the Jedi. Anakin later fights for the Jedi in the Clone Wars.

JEDI KNIGHT
Anakin joins the Jedi Council. Chancellor Palpatine (secretly the Sith Lord Darth Sidious) slowly turns Anakin against his fellow Jedi.

SITH LORD
Anakin betrays the Jedi and joins Palpatine and the dark side. He becomes the evil villain Darth Vader!

"I WILL **FINISH** WHAT YOU STARTED."

KYLO REN TO DARTH VADER'S CHARRED HELMET

ORCE FACTS

ame: Kylo Ren

cupation: Dark side warrior, ght of Ren

filiation: First Order

ecies: Human

meworld: Unknown

ities: Lightsaber skills, side Force user

DARTH SIDIOUS

Sith Lord Darth Sidious always seems to be looking for a new apprentice! He wants to be sure he has the best available.

DARTH MAUL

Sidious' first apprentice is a Zabrak who wields a double-bladed lightsaber. He is defeated by Obi-Wan Kenobi.

COUNT DOOKU

A former Jedi, secretly known as Darth Tyranus, Dooku leads the Separatist Alliance. He is eventually defeated in a lightsaber duel with Yoda.

DARTH VADER

The apprentice that Sidious thought he always wanted— but when Vader's son Luke is discovered, Sidious considers another upgrade...

THE FEROCIOUS
FIRST ORDER

THE SINISTER FIRST ORDER has risen from the ruins of the defeated Empire. Led by the mysterious Supreme Leader Snoke and the dark warrior Kylo Ren, these vile villains are plotting to conquer the galaxy.

NO WAY!

The First Order has built a superweapon even more powerful than the Old Empire's Death Stars— the Starkiller.

FIRST ORDER **LEADERS**

◀ **KYLO REN**
A dark side warrior who acts as the First Order's enforcer.

◀ **CAPTAIN PHASMA**
A chrome-armor-wearing commander who leads the First Order's stormtroopers.

◀ **GENERAL HUX**
A young, ruthless officer in charge of the Starkiller superweapon program.

DOs AND DON'Ts FOR

BEING IN THE FIRST ORDER

DO...
- FOLLOW CAPTAIN PHASMA'S ORDERS
- IRON YOUR UNIFORM
- SPEAK ONLY WHEN SPOKEN TO

DON'T...
- QUESTION AUTHORITY
- RUN AWAY
- ANNOY KYLO REN

"**SUBMIT YOUR BLASTER FOR INSPECTION**."

REAL

Captain Phasma
silver armor is a
made from chro
salvaged from a
Naboo space
yacht.

STRANGE

Almost nothing is kno
about Supreme Leade
He communicates wit
rest of the First Order
via a holographic avat

FORCE FACTS

Name: Phasma

Occupation: Stormtrooper commander

Affiliation: First Order

Species: Human

Homeworld: Unknown

Favorite thing: Destroying her enemies

The ferocious First Order is ready to attack! This grim group has been building weapons and training their forces in the mysterious Unknown Regions. The First Order's troops may look similar to their Imperial predecessors, but their armor is tougher and their weapons are far more powerful.

First Order Forces
TERRIFYING TROOPS

Helmet made from betaplast composite

Armor printing continues on back of torso

Ammunition container

DATA FILE

NAME: First Order Stormtrooper
YEAR: 2015
FIRST SET: 75103 First Order Transporter
NO. OF SETS: 4
PIECES: 5
ACCESSORIES: Blaster

Slit visor reduces the glare from weapon

Ignition chamber and barrel

D-93 Incinerator flamethrower kit

Tough training
The First Order are very strict. Stormtroopers are trained from childhood, which makes them powerful fighters. They are not allowed names and have to be called by their serial numbers.

DATA FILE

NAME: First Order Flametrooper
YEAR: 2016
FIRST SET: 75103 First Order Transporter
NO. OF SETS: 1
PIECES: 13
ACCESSORIES: Flamethrower

DATA FILE

NAME: First Order Snowtrooper
YEAR: 2015
FIRST SET: 75100 First Order Snowspeeder
NO. OF SETS: 1
PIECES: 7
ACCESSORIES: Blaster

Breather tank inlets

Polarized slit visor

Suit heater controls

First Order Snowspeeder (set 75100)

Snowspeeders are used on Starkiller Base. Snowtroopers use them for patrols and to transport supplies between stations.

In the LEGO *Star Wars* theme, this white cloth armor skirt first appeared on the Imperial Snowtrooper

DATA FILE

NAME: First Order TIE Fighter Pilot
YEAR: 2016
FIRST SET: 75101 First Order Special Forces TIE Fighter
NO. OF SETS: 1
PIECES: 4
ACCESSORIES: Blaster

Targeting sensors

Life support gear

Flight suit printing continues onto the back of torso

First Order Special Forces TIE Fighter (set 75101)

TIE fighters have been upgraded since the Imperial era. The First Order's TIE fighters are stronger and more durable. They even have deflector shields.

EVIL
SPEEDERS

THE SITH AND OTHER followers of the dark side are always in a hurry to carry out their horrible deeds. There are Jedi to chase, rebels to crush, and the Resistance to oppose. And for this, they need some super-fast speeders!

WOW!

Snow speeders have special heaters built into their seats to keep snowtroopers toasty warm on the icy surface of the Starkiller superweapon.

TOP 3
Fastest Sith speeders

BRICK-SIZED FACT

There are five versions of Darth Maul's *Bloodfin* speeder. Sith Infiltrator sets include four, and a simpler version comes with 1999's Lightsaber Duel (set 7101).

1 DARTH MAUL'S *BLOODFIN* SPEEDER BIKE
650kph (404mph)

2 COUNT DOOKU'S *FLITKNOT* SPEEDER
634kph (393mph)

3 GENERAL GRIEVOUS' TSMEU-6 WHEEL BIKE
330kph (205mph)

REALLY?!

General Grievous' bike isn't a normal speeder because it rolls on the ground, but neither is the varactyl, Boga, that Obi-Wan uses to chase him on Utapau.

TROOPER **SPEEDERS**

◄ IMPERIAL 614-AvA SPEEDER BIKE

This bike is equipped with two blaster cannons on the front for Imperial pilots and stormtroopers to take down rebels!

IMPERIAL 74-Z SPEEDER BIKE

Used by scout troopers, this bike has a super-powerful boost that allows it to travel long distances in a short amount of time.

IMPERIAL 74-Z SNOW SPEEDER BIKE ▶

Special steering vanes on the front of this snow speeder help the snowtroopers to track down rebels in super-quick time on snowy planets like Hoth.

◄ FIRST ORDER SNOW SPEEDER

First Order snow speeders are bigger, fancier, and more lethal than the rest. They are equipped with rapid-fire blasters, too. The Resistance had better watch out!

FORCE NUMBERS ● ● ● ●

1000m (3281ft)
Firing range of 614-AvA speeder-bike blasters

249 bricks
Make up General Grievous' TSMEU-6 Wheel Bike (set 75040)

2 sets
Feature General Grievous' wheel bike

3 snowtroopers
Fit inside a First Order snow speeder

DK Penguin Random House

Senior Editor Hannah Dolan
Editors Jo Casey, Matt Jones, Clare Millar, Rosie Peet
Senior Designer David McDonald
Senior Slipcase Designer Mark Penfound
Designers Rhys Thomas, Jenny Edwards and Stefan Georgiou
Pre-Production Producer Kavita Varma
Senior Producer Lloyd Robertson
Managing Editor Paula Regan
Design Manager Guy Harvey
Creative Manager Sarah Harland
Art Director Lisa Lanzarini
Publisher Julie Ferris
Publishing Director Simon Beecroft

First American Edition, 2016
Publsihed in the United States by
DK Publishing 345 Hudson Street,
New York, New York 10014
DK, a Division of Penguin Random
House LLC

Contains content previously
published in LEGO® *Star Wars*™
Chronicles of the Force (2016)

002–298872–Jan/17

Page design copyright © 2016
Dorling Kindersley Limited

A catalog record for this book is
available from the Library of Congress.

ISBN 978-5-0010-1396-9

Printed in China

www.LEGO.com/starwars
www.dk.com

A WORLD OF IDEAS:
SEE ALL THERE IS TO KNOW

Dorling Kindersley would like to thank Randi Sørensen, Paul
Hansford, and Martin Leighton Lindhardt at the LEGO Group, and
Jennifer Heddle and Ashley Leonard at Lucasfilm. Thanks also to
Anni Sander for additional text, and Beth Davies, Shari Last, Julia
March, and Helen Murray for editorial assistance.